Preface

Indoor plants should be an integral part of any interior design scheme. Greenery brightens up indoor spaces and is known to improve one's mood.

Indoor plants are popular because they are easy to maintain, provide health benefits, and can be used to complement a number of interior design concepts. Indoor plants are a terrific option for those who don't have enough yard space for an outdoor garden or who live in areas where the winters are bitterly cold.

This book includes all the guidelines on how to grow, care and propagate your indoor plants. This book aims to help those housewives who always worry about decorating their houses with their favorite plants.

Best House plants

Table of Contents

House Plants

Overview

A houseplant is a plant that is cultivated indoors, usually in settings like homes and workplaces, for decorative purposes, but studies have shown that they can also have psychological benefits. They also aid in interior air purification, as some species and the soil-dwelling bacteria associated with them absorb volatile organic pollutants such as benzene, formaldehyde, and trichloroethylene, reducing indoor air pollution. While such contaminants are normally poisonous to humans, they are absorbed by the plant and its soil-dwelling bacteria without causing harm.

Tropical or semi-tropical epiphytes, succulents, and cacti are common houseplants. Houseplants require the right amount of hydration, light, soil, temperature, and humidity. Most house plants will quickly perish if these criteria are not met. In addition, houseplants require the proper fertilizers and pot size.

The Origin of HousePlants

Most houseplants are tropical evergreen species that have developed to thrive in a tropical temperature that varies from 15 to 25 degrees Celsius (60 to 80 degrees Fahrenheit) all year. The natural diversity of plant species and the types utilized as houseplants enable crucial conclusions to be reached regarding their care requirements. Plants in tropical rainforests, unlike those in temperate zones, do not require rest. Their humidity requirements are often quite high. Maintenance benefits from a more detailed understanding of a plant's native vegetation area.

- **Tropical Rainforest**

The majority of plant species cultivated as houseplants are native to the tropical rainforest and its surrounding areas. The day's duration is always around twelve hours. The amount of precipitation falls evenly throughout the year. The average daily temperature varies according to altitude. It is normally between 24 and 28 degrees Celsius all year in tropical forests that are not beyond 600 meters in altitude. Higher-elevation rainforests, often known as tropical mountain forests, can have temperatures as low as 10 degrees Celsius.

The vegetation levels determine the illumination conditions in which different plant species grow. Shade-tolerant plants are usually those that grow near the ground. Climbing plants and epiphytically growing species, on the other hand, demand more light.

Bromeliads, orchids, and philodendrons are examples of tropical rainforest plants that are commonly kept as houseplants. They are perfect for keeping as a houseplant because they usually look great all year long and do not require a specific rest period.

Best House plants

- **Savannah and Desert**

Wet savannah, dry savannah, and thorn bush savannah make up the open savannah environment, which can be found in both the tropics and the subtropics. Plants in this ecosystem have evolved to withstand periods of drought and low humidity. Succulents and cactus are the most common. However, it is crucial to note that many species require cold storage in the winter to flower the following year successfully.

Aside from cactus, aloes, agaves, crassula, echeveria, euphorbia, and sansevieria have become popular houseplants.

- **Subtropics**

The subtropics are known for their variable day lengths that fluctuate with the seasons, as well as a warm winter with plenty of rain. Precipitation occurs only on rare occasions during the summer, and temperatures can reach dangerously high levels. Houseplants from this vegetative zone include myrtles and oleanders, as well as several ficus species.

- **Temperate zone**

Only a few species of plants that are kept as indoor plants are native to temperate climatic zones. Cultivated ivy, as well as Saxifraga stolonifera and Carexbrunnea, are typical specimens. They can only survive if they keep themselves as cool as possible.

Health Benefits of Houseplants

An indoor garden may be a haven from the outside world and a source of tremendous joy for many people. Introducing specific plants into your home, whether you live in a little apartment or a large house, will start to improve your health and overall pleasure. Plants can assist with loneliness and melancholy by increasing your mood and creating a peaceful living space: caring for a living thing gives us a purpose and is fulfilling, especially when you see that live thing bloom and thrive. There are several benefits of house plants that are given below.

Happy Blooms

Plants can not only brighten your environment, but they can also improve your mood. Employees who work in workplaces with plants have a better attitude toward their jobs, are less worried, and take fewer sick days. Flowers, in particular, are a great mood booster. So add some blooms to your space, such as a lipstick plant or a new bouquet, and watch if your mood improves.

Air Purifiers

VOCs are emitted by a variety of indoor objects, including carpets, paint, cleaners, printer toners and inks, and many others (VOCs). They can accumulate in the air, irritate your eyes and skin, aggravate asthma, or make breathing difficult. Houseplants can absorb VOCs. English ivy, asparagus fern, and dragon tree are all good air scrubbers.

Herbs for a Better Digestive System

Mint can aid with bloating, gas, and other digestive issues after a meal. Peppermint and spearmint are two common kinds that can be grown in containers (essential in mint juleps). Basil, another cooking herb, might also aid in settling your stomach. Steep the leaves in boiling water for a while.

Relaxing Lavender

For generations, this aromatic purple shrub has been used as a herbal treatment. Aromatherapy can be achieved by inhaling lavender oil or massaging it into your scalp. Tea can be made by boiling the leaves. According to research, it may help you relax and reduce anxiety. However, further evidence is required.

Restful Sleep

Carbon dioxide is taken in by plants, and they emit oxygen. It's a process called photosynthesis that allows them to convert sunshine into food. Some plants, such as gerbera daisies, continue to release oxygen even after the sun has set. If you place a few bright pots in your bedroom,

the increased oxygen may help you sleep better.

Stress Relief

Do you feel the strain of daily responsibilities? Add a snake plant or a heart-leaf philodendron to your decor. It might assist you in unwinding. Several studies have evaluated people's blood pressure, heart rate, and the stress hormone cortisol while they were performing a difficult activity or dealing with mental stress. People feel more relaxed when they are in the presence of plants.

Sharper Focus

Plants can help you improve your test scores, focus better on your duties, and boost your memory. Students in classrooms with three potted plants outperformed students in schools without greenery on math, spelling, reading, and science assessments. Bring home a golden pothos or a bamboo palm, and you might just be able to cross something off your to-do list.

Healing time is Reduced.

Visiting a loved one in the hospital with a bouquet of flowers or potted plants can be more than simply a considerate gesture. It could really help people heal faster. According to researchers, people who had surgery recovered faster if they had plants in their room or a glimpse of nature from their window. When they were surrounded by greenery, they also endured pain better and required fewer drugs. A peace lily or an orchid is a good choice.

Spider Plants for Moisture

Furnaces and air conditioners, especially in the winter, can deplete indoor humidity. This can make you more susceptible to contracting a cold or the flu, as well as itching your skin. Houseplants help to keep the air wet. According to one study, a collection of spider plants increased the relative humidity in a bedroom from 20% to a more comfortable 30%.

Aloe Vera

Best House plants

What's green, spiky, and decorative all over? That's aloe vera, a succulent houseplant that's as attractive as it is useful. This tolerant desert native puts up with careless waterers and inexperienced gardeners while also providing a hidden benefit in the form of thick, pointed leaves. When applied directly to minor burns, the gel inside serves as a typical sunburn soother, easing redness.

Give your new potted pal plenty of bright, indirect light and a good watering every two weeks, and it'll appreciate you - and perhaps even reward you with new plant "babies." Get the things you'll need first, and then read on for a complete guide to aloe vera plant care.

How to Grow Aloe Vera

Many home gardeners prefer aloe because of its resilience and tolerance for infrequent watering. Plant aloe in a terra cotta container with well-drained soil to keep it happy. Mix equal parts sand and potting soil or purchase a succulent specialty mix. Terra cotta dries more quickly than plastic or glazed vessels.

If your aloe starts to tip over due to its weight, repot it, but otherwise, don't worry about giving it a lot of room. This plant thrives in confined spaces.

Make sure your aloe is in a bright, sunny location. It will go dormant and stop developing if this is not done. Water the plant heavily every two weeks or so until the soil is completely dry. Because this is a desert plant, moistening the soil will cause the roots to rot. Limp or brown leaves are another indicator that you've gone too far with the H20.

You can bring your potted plant outside for the summer if you want, but don't put it in bright sunlight straight soon. To avoid overexposure, gradually move it to a brighter location every few days.

How to Care Aloe Vera

Your aloe will occasionally produce a tall stem of miniature, bell-shaped flowers as a bonus after the blossoms have faded. Cut the stem at the base.

Better yet, aloe plants develop new, smaller plants that are ideal for propagation. If you come upon one of these "babies," remove the Earth and pry apart the roots of the several plants, replanting in different containers.

You can start your own aloe plants by clipping off a few leaves if you want to present aloe plants to pals. Trim the leaf tip to about 3 inches and place the trimmed ends in a container of potting mix. While not all of them will develop new leaves at the base, some will. Before repotting this new plant, wait until it has grown a few inches.

- **Light**

Aloe Vera has to be in a bright, indirect light environment: Its delicate skin can be burned by direct sunlight.

- **Soil**

The soil must be well-draining. Aloe often grows on slopes in its natural habitat, ensuring good drainage. You can purchase a particular cactus potting soil or mix in some perlite or coarse sand to make your own mix to ensure drainage in a pot.

- Water

Aloe can withstand drought, but it prefers to be watered on a regular basis, with the soil allowed to dry completely between waterings. The leaves will shrink and pucker somewhat if the plant is kept too dry for too long. When hydrated, they will recover, but continuous stress, such as drought or excess water, will cause the leaves to be yellow and die.

During the rainy season, don't give the plants any extra water. Most aloes go dormant in the winter and don't need any water as long as they have enough water throughout the growing season. Consider planting your aloe in gravel or stones if your climate is wet throughout the winter. They'll let the water flow away.

- Temperature and Humidity

Aloe Vera thrives in temperatures between 55 and 85 degrees Fahrenheit but will withstand temperatures as low as 40 degrees Fahrenheit. It is unable to withstand frost.

- **Fertilizer**

Aloe vera does not require a lot of fertility in the soil. It should be sufficient to feed once a year, in the spring, with houseplant fertilizers.

- **Pruning**

Aloe vera does not require a lot of fertility in the soil. It should be sufficient to feed once a year, in the spring, with houseplant fertilizers.

Propagation of Aloe Vera

Offsets are also known as pups because they are the parent plant's offspring. When an Aloe Vera matures, they normally sprout from the side of the stem. As you know, it's been neglected, lacks soil, has outgrown its container, has offsets and has a mother of thousands plant growing next to it for some reason.

1. Remove The Plant From The Pot

When removing the plant from the pot, tilt it to the side while holding the main stem (as much of the plant as possible) or tip it upside down if the plant isn't too large. If the plant does not come out, squeeze the pot's sides, tap the sides, or tap the pot's rim upside down on the edge of a table or low wall.

When you take the pot out of the pot, remove the old soil from the roots and make sure that all of the roots are healthy. Remove any that have turned brown, and cut away any diseased leaves with a sharp knife. To make the plant more appealing, clip the leaves close to the stem; otherwise, half a leaf shoots out with no tip and does not seem as good.

2. Separate Offsets

Some offsets require cutting away, while others can simply be pulled away from the parent plant. They're easy to pull away if you're repotting, but if the parent plant is staying in its present container, you'll need to make a cut with a sharp knife. Keep the offsets roots intact when making a separation.

3. Unhealthy Leaf Removal

Now remove the unhealthy or unwanted Leeds

4. Offsets Removed

It is recommended that offsets be removed when they are about a quarter of the size of the parent plant, but in this case, it appears that removing all of them, repotting, trimming, and trying to get as many of them rooted and growing as possible is the best option. We don't worry if one or two are lost, as long as the parent plant is flourishing well.

5. Planting

Find a good size container (with drainage holes), fill it loosely with potting mix, and then use your finger to make a deep and broad enough hole for the plant's lower stem and roots to be planted. Fill the pot with soil and gently press the soil down with your fingers once the plant and roots have been placed in the hole. This will allow the plant to be firm enough not to tumble over as it grows. We fill a pot with soil until it reaches approximately a millimeter from the top.

6. Watering

All that remains is to water the plants. Give them a good watering until water starts to drip out of the drainage holes in the bottom. After you've finished watering, continue with the standard routine for watering Aloes and caring for them.

Spider plant

Best House plants

The spider plant is one of the easiest plants to keep alive, so you may do it even if your fingers are purple, blue, or yellow instead of green. It enjoys a glass of water once or twice a week, but if you forget about it for a long, it will forgive you. As a result, the spider plant is an excellent office companion. The spear-shaped leaves of the spider plant can grow to be 45cm long. The petite, exquisite white flowers, which resemble lilies, grow on stalks from the plant's center. Young plants develop on the stem and can be simply removed and placed in their own pot. The roots of the spider plant are thick and fleshy, and they hold a lot of moisture so that they can go without water for a long time.

The spider plant originated as a groundcover in the South African tropical rainforest, where 65 different varieties can be found. It belongs to the asparagus family and belongs to the same genus as the agave plant. In the nineteenth century, it made its way into our living rooms.

How to Grow Spider Plant

Grow in a potting mix that is soil-based and drains nicely. Spider plants prefer a consistent amount of moisture; they don't enjoy being too dry or too wet.

Plants should be kept in bright to mild, indirect sunlight. Direct, hot sunlight is not good for spider plants since it can burn their leaves, resulting in brown tips and patches.

Spider plants grow swiftly and might quickly outgrow their pots. Plan on repotting a spider plant every other year or so.

During the summer, spider plants can be cultivated as annuals outside. As long as they are kept out of direct sunshine, they look great around the edge of a container or bed.

How to Care Spider Plant

Because of their cascading foliage and long stems with plantlets, spider plants are frequently planted in containers as hanging plants. They're also stunning when planted atop columns. If you set their container on something instead of hanging it, be sure the long leaves don't get crushed, and the long plantlet stems don't get too heavy to pull the pot over. Spider plants do nicely in outdoor planters and as ground cover plants in warm regions.

The most time-consuming aspect of spider plant care is usually regular watering. Plan to fertilizer on a regular basis during the growing season (spring to fall). And, if your plant's roots have outgrown the container, repot it as needed.

- **Light**

Spider plants tend to grow in the light shade outside. They can withstand a lot of shade, but their growth will be stunted. The leaves can be scorched by direct sunshine. Inside, a bright window with indirect sunlight is great.

- **Soil**

These plants can thrive in a wide range of soil types, although they prefer loose, loamy soil with good drainage. They like a pH that is rather neutral, but they may survive soil that is slightly acidic to slightly alkaline. The browning of leaf tips might be caused by a high quantity of salts in the soil.

- **Water**

Spider plants prefer soil that is somewhat damp but not saturated. Overwatering can lead to root rot, which will eventually destroy the plant. Fluoride and chlorine in water cause browning of the leaf tips in some plants. If at all possible, water container plants using rainwater or distilled water.

- **Temperature and Humidity**

Spider plants thrive in warm, humid environments. Temperatures below 50 degrees Fahrenheit are unsuitable for them. When grown indoors, they should be shielded from draughts and air conditioning vents. Furthermore, if the humidity is too low, the leaf tips can discolor. Misting the plant on a regular basis can aid in maintaining proper humidity levels.

- **Fertilizer**

A moderate amount of fertilizer is preferred by these plants. Brown leaf tips can be caused by too much fertilizer, whereas sluggish growth might be caused by too little fertilizer. 1 During the growing season, use all-purpose granular or water-soluble fertilizers as directed on the label. Depending on the size of your plant, you may need to adjust the amount.

Propagation of Spider Plant

Growing spider plants from babies is the most popular technique of propagation, and it can be done in a few different ways. While they're still linked to the mother plant, you can root them in soil. You may also break them off, and either roots them in water or propagate them in a propagation box. Depending on the spider plant propagation method you use, starting spider plants from cuttings can take anywhere from a few days to a number of weeks.

1. **Taking a cutting from spider Plant**

Before taking spider plant cuttings, wait until the babies have started forming their own beginning root structures. If the spider plant babies don't have roots or only have little nubs, you should wait until they're a little older. Once you've determined that a plantlet is ready to proliferate, you can cut it free from the mother. When you disturb the babies, they may come.

It actually doesn't matter where you cut the spider plant pups from their mother. However, we prefer to trim them as close to the spider plantlets as possible to avoid an unsightly stem sticking out. You obtain a great clean-cut. Make sure to use a sterile pair of precision clippers.

Because nothing new will grow on the long stem after you remove the baby, you can prune it back to the bottom of the next one up or all the way to the main plant.

2.   Rooting Spider Plant Babies in Water

Placing the babies in water until new roots begin to grow is the easiest technique to propagate spider plants. The main disadvantages of rooting cuttings in water are that the plantlet may decay and that when transplanted into the dirt, it may experience shock. When the babies are rooted in water, they are weaker, and it can take a long time for them to recover after being planted in dirt.

If you're having trouble with spider plant babies dying after potting them up, you should try one of the other two rooting procedures next time. Cut or pinch any leaves growing at the base of the plantlet or under the roots before putting them in water. Any greenery that becomes submerged in water roots. To root my spider plant spiderettes, we like to use a deep, transparent container. However, only enough water should be in the vase to cover the roots of the infant plant.

The plantlet will rot if it is submerged in water that is too deep. The plantlets are kept erect, and the foliage is kept out of the water by using a tall, slender vase.

3.   Rooting Baby Spider Plant in a Propagation Chamber

It's simple to keep the humidity level high when propagating plant cuttings in a propagation chamber. Humidity aids the spiderettes in their rooting process. Baby plants planted in this manner are also stronger and less likely to succumb to transplant shock than those rooted in water.

You can purchase a propagation kit or a micro greenhouse system or build your own propagation box from scratch. If you decide to make your own, adding bottom heat can greatly expedite the process. You may also try making a little greenhouse by placing a plastic bag over the plantlet and dirt.

4.   Propagating Spider Plant Babies While They are Still Attached

You don't have to worry about transplant shock if you root spider plantlets while they're still linked to the mother plant. When spider plants are propagated in this manner, the babies are stronger from the start. However, this procedure is more challenging since spiderettes that are still attached to the mother may not root as readily as those that are removed. You may use standard potting soil or the same mild rooting mix you'd use in a propagation box for this strategy. Simply place a pot of soil next to the mother plant and plant the baby's beginning.

5. Rooting Spider Plant Babies in Water

Placing the babies in water until new roots begin to grow is the easiest technique to propagate spider plants. The main disadvantages of rooting cuttings in water are that the plantlet may decay and that when transplanted into the dirt, it may experience shock. When the babies are rooted in water, they are weaker, and it can take a long time for them to recover after being planted in dirt.

If you're having trouble with spider plant babies dying after potting them up, you should try one of the other two rooting procedures next time. Cut or pinch any leaves growing at the base of the plantlet or under the roots before putting them in water. Any greenery that becomes submerged in water roots. To root my spider plant spiderettes, we like to use a deep, transparent container. However, only enough water should be in the vase to cover the roots of the infant plant.

The plantlet will rot if it is submerged in water that is too deep. The plantlets are kept erect, and the foliage is kept out of the water by using a tall, slender vase.

6. Rooting Baby Spider Plant in a Propagation Chamber

It's simple to keep the humidity level high when propagating plant cuttings in a propagation chamber. Humidity aids the spiderettes in their rooting process. Baby plants that are planted this manner are also stronger and less likely to succumb to transplant shock than those that are rooted in water.

You can purchase a propagation kit or a micro greenhouse system, or you can build your own propagation box from scratch. If you decide to make your own, adding bottom heat can greatly expedite the process. You may also try making a little greenhouse by placing a plastic bag over the plantlet and dirt.

7. Propagating Spider Plant Babies While They are Still Attached

You don't have to worry about transplant shock if you root spider plantlets while they're still linked to the mother plant. When spider plants are propagated in this manner, the babies are stronger from the start. However, this procedure is more challenging since spiderettes that are still attached to the mother may not root as readily as those that are removed. You may use standard potting soil or the same mild rooting mix you'd use in a propagation box for this strategy. Simply place a pot of soil next to the mother plant and plant the baby's beginning roots in it.

8.   Transplanting Spider Plant Babies

Before potting spider plant babies, let the plantlets grow multiple new roots. Then you can put them up with regular potting soil. Water the rooted baby thoroughly after planting it in its own pot, allowing the excess water to drain out the bottom.

Maintain an even moisture level in the soil until the plant has established itself in its new pot, but don't overwater it. To aid recovery, you may wish to wet it daily with a plant mister or keep it in a humid location like a bathroom or kitchen at first. When you see new growth, the plant has established, and you can stop fussing with it. After they've established themselves, juvenile spider plants require the same care as mature spider plants.

Best House plants

Monstera Deliciosa

Best House plants

Few plants have as much drama and personality as Monstera deliciosa and its cousins when it comes to making a botanical statement about living life on your own terms. However, these exotic tropical appear difficult to cultivate and care for; knowing how to develop and care for monsteras is an easy and rewarding process. Here's all you need to know about monsteras, whether they're on your wish list or already in your garden. Your monstera may not appear to be a vine, but it is. These stunning creatures are native to Central America's tropical rainforests, where they soar to incredible heights from the jungle floor. Although the majority of monsteras have a similar appearance, narrowing down your choice is part of the fun:

The most common monstera on the market is Monstera deliciosa, popularly known as the Swiss-cheese plant. Its huge, heart-shaped leaves produce large holes along the main leaf vein, and large leaf splits around the outside margin when mature — and given enough light.

Monkey mask, Monstera adansonii, is a less frequent species. The outer edge of its arrow-shaped leaves does not split. The holes, on the other hand, remain within the leaf borders. Monstera obliqua is a rare plant that is rarely available for purchase, while mislabeled specimens are widespread. Monstera adansonii has narrower, thinner leaves and a higher percentage of leaf holes than Monstera adansonii.

All monsteras belong to the Araceae botanical family, which is harmful to pets if eaten. If you have pets, teach them not to consume houseplants or plant pieces. Contact your veterinarian straight once if your pet eats monstera leaves or stems.

How to Grow Monstera deliciosa

Monsteras, which are native to the tropics, grow to incredible heights because of aerial roots. Plants' normal roots anchor them to the ground, whereas aerial roots anchor them to trees, walls, and other above-ground surfaces, allowing them to climb.

Monsteras in your home don't grow to the same heights as those in the jungle, but they do grow in the same way. By providing a moss pole for support, you can help your monstera achieve its goals. As your monstera flies, the aerial roots will develop into the moss and anchor it.

Monstera deliciosa are long-lived plants that can reach 10 to 15 feet tall and 8 feet.

How to Care Monstera deliciosa

Monstera deliciosa thrives year-round in warm, humid climates and is hardy in USDA Zones 10 through 12. Plant it in part shade in well-draining soil when planting it outside. If the soil in your area is naturally salty, take it to the patio or indoors. If you use balanced fertilizers three or four times a year, the plant can reach a height of 10 feet or more. Choose a deep pot with plenty of drainage holes if it'll be used as a houseplant.

- **Light**

This evergreen enjoys bright, indirect sunlight and steady temperatures of 65 to 75 degrees Fahrenheit. In the summer, too

Best House plants

Broad inside, with leaves measuring 18 inches across or more, if given the correct circumstances and support. Variegated monsteras grow much more slowly indoors and rarely reach that size.

Expect your monstera's leaf holes and splits to change considerably as it ages. Leaf holes can evolve to dramatic split leaves depending on the plant type and growing conditions. It's extremely vital to have the right amount of light. Low light reduces the formation of holes and splits.

much direct light can cause the foliage to burn. Set indoor plants outside in direct sunshine at least once a year to encourage luxuriant growth.

The Swiss cheese plant thrives in the full shadow of deep woodlands and the semi-shade of light woodlands when grown outdoors.

- **Soil**

It requires peat-based potting material to be established in a container. It grows well in light sandy, medium loamy, and heavy clay soils with an acid or neutral pH outside. Despite this, it prefers well-drained, somewhat damp soil.

- **Water**

During the growing season, give the plant one to two weekly watering's. Continually add water until the surplus drains through the drainage holes. Because the plant has used all of the water it requires, do not return the surplus water to the container. Between watering's, the soil should be allowed to dry gradually. In the fall and winter, only water on occasion. Mist the vegetation with a spray bottle of demineralized water or rainfall to boost humidity indoors.

- **Fertilizer**

Use a balanced liquid of 20-20-20 fertilizers every few weeks during the growing season for indoor plants if needed or desired. In a gallon of water, dissolve 1/2 teaspoon of fertilizers. Use diluted fertilizers instead of water on a regular basis. Pour the mixture into the soil until it starts to drain through the drainage holes. Because the plant has used all of the diluted fertilizers, it will not be able to use the excess that drains away.

- **Pruning**

Trim aerial roots if they become too rowdy for the space; nonetheless, tucking them back into the pot is preferable. Their roots, unlike those of several other houseplants, don't damage surfaces. Trimming works well on stems and leaves, and they can be used for propagation.

Propagation of Monstera Deliciosa

A Monstera deliciosa can be propagated using a variety of ways and components of the plant. Nodes, aerial roots, and even seeds can fall within this category. Let's take a look at each of these plant elements to see what role they might play in propagation.

Seed

While it is possible to grow a monstera plant from a seed, the seeds can only be harvested from a fruiting plant.

Monstera deliciosa produces the Mexican breadfruit, and the seeds are actually embedded in the fruit, making it edible (and quite tasty!). However, because Monstera deliciosa rarely bears fruit indoors, this may not be the greatest method for propagating an indoor monstera. However, if you have a fruiting plant outside, go ahead and collect those seeds!

Monstera seeds can also be purchased and germinated like any other seed. However, be wary with con artists. Make sure you examine independent reviews and ratings of any vendor you're thinking about buying seeds from to ensure they have a strong reputation for sending out high-quality seeds.

Seeds can be found at online retailers, as well as on eBay and in Etsy shops. You should anticipate paying somewhere between $1 and $2 per seed. If you already have the patience and equipment, this can be a cost-effective approach to raise some beautiful monstera plants!

We strongly advise against purchasing purported multicolored monstera seeds. This is because it's impossible to predict whether a monstera seed will create a variegated plant, even if it came from a variegated plant. Buying a clipping from a variegated plant is the only way to ensure variegation.

Here's what to do if you do manage to get your hands on some genuine monstera seeds:

Step 1-Prep

Start your seeds right away because they won't last long after they've been taken from the fruit. Soak your seeds in lukewarm water for 12-24 hours before planting, and keep them somewhere warm.

Step 2-Plant

Fill a shallow container halfway with dirt and poke a small hole in the medium. Place the seed in the hole, bury it, and thoroughly water it. To speed up the germination process, add some liquid rooting hormones like Propagation Promoter to the water.

Step 3-Cover and Wait

Keep your seeds warm (at least 70 degrees Fahrenheit) and covered with a clear plastic covering to maintain a high level of humidity around them. To give the seeds some energy without scorching them, keep the soil wet and in a place with moderate light.

It's a good idea to keep your seedlings on a heating mat to help them germinate faster.

If you want to make things easier, you can buy whole seed starting kits that include everything you'll need!

Aerial Root

It's wonderful news for your propagation attempts if your monstera plant has aerial roots! Because aerial roots grow near nodes, putting one in your stem cutting or air layering near an aerial root can help your plant generate new roots faster.

If you have a nice aerial root on a stem with some healthy new leaves, air layering can be a useful strategy to attempt because the risk of shock and infection is reduced.

To do this, you'll need a few supplies:

- Sphagnum moss
- String or twist ties
- Plastic wrap
- A spray bottle filled with clean water
- Optional: liquid rooting hormone such as Propagation Promoter

To air layer, find a node or aerial root just below the leaf you want to propagate on your monstera plant. It should resemble a small brown bump or growth on the opposite side of a leaf's stem.

Make a small cut around the node's stem using a sharp, clean knife or pruning shears. This small wound will cause the plant to focus its energy in that direction, allowing new roots to sprout! Use a cotton ball to dab a little liquid rooting hormone on the injury to kick-start root growth.

Wrap the cut, node, and stem in dampened (but not drenched and dripping) sphagnum moss, then loosely wrap the wad of moss in plastic wrap to allow for airflow. Using string or twist knots, secure the entire thing.

To keep the moss damp, loosen the plastic wrap every couple of days and spritz it with water. You should observe brand-new aerial roots developing around the region in a few months!

Remove the moss and plastic and cut that part of the stem and leaves off the plant, being careful to include your new roots! And place in a pot when the roots are an inch or two long.

You have a brand-new monstera plant. Care for your new plant as you would a mature monstera.

Stem Cutting

Stem cuttings are the most popular approach to reproduce a monstera plant. Cutting a section of the plant and helping it to grow its own roots so it may be planted is what this entails.

Find a healthy, growing portion of your monstera plant with at least one healthy leaf and a node to do this. Cut the part off the monstera, including the node, with a clean pair of shears. You can also spread healthy leaves from nodes you trim off your monstera to keep its size under control.

Place the cutting in a clear glass of clean water with a small amount of Propagation Promoter and place it somewhere bright. Be patient and change the water at least once a week. You should have roots in a few months. You can put your monstera in soil once the roots are an inch or two long.

You can also directly put your fresh cutting into the soil. Keep the pot in a light spot and the dirt moist. To ward off diseases and give the young roots a boost of nutrients, mix a little liquid Propagation Promoter into the water.

While rooting cuttings in water is a more straightforward procedure, we prefer it to reduce infection risk. Plus, you'll be able to observe the development of your new baby roots!

Leaf Node

Because nodes are where new roots will form, this is the single most crucial element of propagating a monstera plant. You'll need a node whether you're spreading by cuttings or air layering. While aerial roots and nodes are connected, an aerial root is not required for propagation. It's only a node!

In fact, even if there isn't a leaf, you can propagate from a stem with a node! Although your odds of success are limited, a stem with a node can take root and begin to generate new leaves. It's all about the nodes in this game!

Is it Possible to Grow a Monstera Leaf?

Nope. If you want to propagate your monstera plant from a leaf cutting, make sure it has a node because that's where new roots will develop. It will not take root if you try to propagate a leaf from a node.

23

Philodendron

Philodendron (genus Philodendron) is a genus of over 450 species of stout-stemmed climbing herbs from the Araceae family that are native to tropical America. Many species start as vines before evolving into epiphytes (plants that live upon other plants). Young philodendrons are attractive potted plants for homes and offices since they are accustomed to the low light levels of rainforests.

Philodendron foliage is normally green, but it can also be coppery, crimson, or purplish; parallel leaf veins are usually green, but they can also be red or white. The leaves' shape, size, and texture vary greatly depending on the plant's species and maturity. The berry is white to orange in color. The differences between the juvenile and adult phases make it nearly hard to distinguish between distinct kinds of tiny plants.

Most philodendrons are excellent climbers, wrapping their modified roots around tree trunks to grow higher. Once they've made it to the top of the canopy, they frequently convert into epiphytes. Secondary hemiepiphytes are plants with this lifestyle. Hemiepiphyte seedlings, unlike most plants, do not develop toward the sun; instead, they grow toward the trunk of a tree. They switch to a light-seeking approach and use modified roots to rise to the top.

The stem eventually dies at the tree's base, cutting off its connection to the soil. Only the top of the plant retains a little stalk. The philodendron may wander further if it reaches the treetop. If its current location is too shady, it can relocate by creating more stem and growing in front while dying behind. It can drop new roots to the ground if the area becomes too dry. Many philodendrons, unlike most epiphytes, do not die if they fall to the ground. They merely start their ascent all over again.

How to Grow Philodendron

Even in less-than-ideal conditions, philodendrons can thrive. If they're well-cared-for, however, you'll be rewarded with a steady stream of new growth.

It's all about finding the right balance of water, nutrients, environment, and sunlight, just like any other plant.

Soil Needs

Moisture management is one of the most crucial aspects of philodendron care.

These plants demand well-draining soil that is continuously damp but not wet.

How to Care Philodendron

When caring for an indoor philodendron plant, try to recreate the plant's native tropical habitat. Warmth and moisture should be plentiful near a sunny window. Put philodendron houseplants outside in a shady place to get some fresh air and natural light during the summer. Direct sunlight should be avoided because it can damage their fragile foliage.

Wipe your plant's leaves down with a moist towel on a frequent basis to keep them looking and operating their best. There are no severe pest or disease problems with these plants. However, they are prone to aphids, mealybugs, scale, thrips and spiders

Best House plants

Even in less-than-ideal conditions, philodendrons can thrive. If they're well-cared-for, however, you'll be rewarded with a steady stream of new growth.

It's all about finding the right balance of water, nutrients, environment, and sunlight, just like any other plant.

Soil Needs

Moisture management is one of the most crucial aspects of philodendron care.

These plants demand well-draining soil that is continuously damp but not wet.

When the soil is overly damp, the roots may struggle to absorb nutrients and oxygen, making it easier for detrimental bacteria and fungi to take hold.

Philodendrons prefer a slightly acidic pH range of 5.0-6.0.

The excellent, slightly acidic, the well-draining growing medium comprises one part of ordinary potting soil, one part peat moss, and one part perlite.

Container Selection

In order to keep plants from becoming waterlogged, it's also important to choose the correct container size.

Choosing a huge pot in the mistaken belief that the plant would grow into it is a common rookie mistake. Your container shouldn't be so small that the plant becomes root-bound, but it also shouldn't be so large that the plant doesn't get enough water from the soil.

mites, which are common houseplant pests. Use a natural insecticidal soap or horticultural oil to get rid of pests.

- **Light**

Partially shaded areas are ideal for philodendrons. Under a tropical canopy, they would naturally receive dappled light rather than direct sunlight. Set them up near a window that receives bright, indirect light indoors. If there isn't enough light, the plant will become lanky, and there will be a lot of gaps between the leaves. However, too much light can cause a large number of leaves to become yellow at once. The yellowing of a few leaves is usually due to normal aging.

- **Soil**

Philodendrons prefer organically rich, loose potting soil. The soil must be well-drained. It's best to replenish your philodendron's soil every couple of years or so if you have one in a container. Salts that collect in the soil as a result of watering are toxic to these plants, causing leaf browning and yellowing. You can flush out some of the salts by thoroughly watering the container until water pours out of the drainage holes on a regular basis. However, the soil will eventually need to be replenished.

- **Water**

These plants prefer a modest amount of moisture in the soil. When the top inch of soil has dried out, water it. Overwatering and underwatering can both cause the leaves to droop, so look at the soil dryness rather than the leaves to determine when it's time to water. Philodendrons don't like sitting in wet soil since it causes root rot.

Best House plants

Plant roots should occupy roughly a third of the pot, according to a good rule of thumb. This will allow it to flourish while also preventing root rot, a fungal disease that thrives in moist, oversaturated soil.

If growing outside, make sure the container has drainage holes so that excess rains may escape, and avoid planting in hard clay soils.

Drought tolerance is slightly higher in non-climbing variations than in vining species. Reduce the amount of water you use for indoor plants, especially in the winter.

- **Temperature and Humidity**

Philodendrons' temperature tolerance varies depending on the species. They shouldn't be exposed to temperatures below 55 degrees Fahrenheit in general. Cool draughts, such as those from an air-conditioning vent, are protected from them when they are indoors. Because these plants prefer humidity, you may need to increase humidity around your philodendron if you live in a dry region. You can do this by misting the plant with water from a spray bottle every few days. You can also set the container on a tray of pebbles filled with water, making sure that the container's bottom does not come into contact with the water, which could cause root rot.

- **Fertilizer**

In the spring and summer, apply balanced fertilizers to your plant once a month. In the fall and winter, limit feeding to every six to eight weeks. If your plant isn't getting enough nutrients, it will grow slowly, and its leaves will be smaller than usual.

- **Pruning**

Cut back your philodendron vines with sterilizing pruning shears or scissors if they become too long or lanky. In the spring or summer, this is the perfect time to do it. To remove fading leaves and trim spindly growth, you can safely give your philodendron a modest trim at any time of year. Just above a leaf node is the finest place to cut. Use your stem cuttings to propagate your plants.

Propogation of Philodendrons

Philodendrons are a genus of tropical plants with over 200 species. Commonly grown as houseplants are fiddle leaf philodendrons (Philodendron panduriforme), heart-leaf philodendrons (Philodendron scandens), and tree philodendrons (Philodendron bipinnatifidum). Although they are sensitive to cold weather, these plants can be cultivated as perennials in USDA plant hardiness zones 10 through 12. It is relatively simple to propagate them.

Tip & Stem Cuttings

Philodendron stem cuttings are easy to root. Many may be rooted in a glass jar or a vase of water, but if you root them in moist perlite or peat moss, they will establish a stronger root system. You can root numerous plants from one vine because philodendrons can be propagated via tip or stem cuttings. Cut 2 to 3 inches from the end of the vine for tip cuttings so that it contains the young leaves at the tip. Remove a 10-inch vine and cut it into multiple 2 to 3-inch parts for stem cuttings. Place the cuttings in a vase of water and set them in a warm spot to root in water. If not, dip the cutting's basal end (the end that faces the main plant) in the rooting hormone and place it in moist potting soil. Cover the pots with plastic wrap and place them under a bright, indirect light source. For best root production, keep the soil temperature between 70 and 75 degrees Fahrenheit. Maintain a moist but not saturated soil until the roots have been established. Gently tug on the cutting to see if it has formed roots. The roots are sufficiently established if it resists your efforts. Transfer the new plants to their own containers.

Dividing Philodendrons

Overgrown or mature philodendron can be divided to produce new plants quickly. Because each part has a well-established root system, new growth emerges quickly, and the new plant usually flourishes. To separate the roots, water the plant thoroughly in the morning to hydrate and loosen the soil. This facilitates division and offers the moisture your philodendron requires to counteract the stress of transplanting. Remove the plant from the container and gently separate the roots into two or more pieces, each with at least two branches. Set aside the division for potting in fresh soil and replant the main plant in the original container.

Air Layering

Philodendrons that have become overgrown and droopy are ideal candidates for air layering. Remove the leaves 3 to 4 inches above and below a leaf node from a part of the stem. Cut a 1-inch slit in the plant's stem using a sharp, sterilized knife. Angle the cut upwards until it reaches the stem's center, but don't sever the stem. Insert a toothpick into the slit so that the width of the toothpick keeps the slit open and the ends of the toothpick protrude on either side of the stem. The wound will not heal as a result of this.

To encourage excellent root development, dust the cut with rooting hormone. Wrap the incision in two handfuls of moist peat moss and cover it with plastic wrap, taking care to seal the edges to prevent moisture loss. Using tape or string, secure the plastic and peat moss in place. Keep an eye out for new roots forming inside the plastic. When the bag is full of new roots, cut the new plant free of the stem and plant it in the soil.

Potting Media for Transplanting

Philodendrons prefer loose, well-drained, organically rich soil. They can be planted in peat moss, a mix of peat moss and perlite, or a homemade potting medium made from equal parts perlite, peat moss, and either all-purpose potting soil or compost. Because they are too heavy, compact quickly with repeated watering, and drain slowly, all-purpose potting soil or garden loam is not suggested for plants in containers.

Transplanting Cuttings or Divisions

Fill your plant pot or container with a fresh potting medium to about three-fourths full. Place the rooted cutting or division in the plant pot and spread the roots out over the soil. Fill up the space around the roots with Earth. Adjust the cutting or division such that the crown, or the point where the roots and stem meet, rests on the soil line. To secure the plant, firm the Earth down with your hands. Place the new plants in a bright, indirect light-filled area away from direct sunlight.

Birds Nest Ferns

Best House plants

Asplenium nidus, or Bird's Nest Fern, is one of numerous popular and attractive ferns grown as houseplants. Ferns such as this one thrive in the type of light and milder temperatures that North-facing windows provide.

The Bird's Nest Fern will reward you with a large number of naturally glossy leaves grouped in a circular arrangement that resembles a bird's nest (hence the common name for these houseplants). Because bathrooms and often used kitchens have a steamy atmosphere, they're very suitable indoor plants for them.

This is vital since a Bird Nest Fern needs humidity to thrive indoors. They may survive and thrive in a standard room, but for that extra shine and size, you'll need to spray on a regular basis. If you don't have time to spray your plants, the Birds Nest Fern is a great plant to keep in a home terrarium or glass bottle garden. These confined spaces produce naturally moist and protected habitats that many plants, including most ferns, thrive in.

How to Grow birds nest ferns in a garden

Select a location in the garden that receives part shade to filtered sun and is shaded from the afternoon sun. Dig in Yates Dynamic Lifter Soil Improver & Plant Fertilizer to thoroughly prepare the planting area.

Dig the planting hole twice as broad as the root-ball and to the same depth. Take the plant out of its container and gently tease the roots.

Backfill the hole with Earth, carefully firming it down. Form a raised or doughnut-shaped ring of dirt around the plant's root zone's perimeter. This allows water to stay where it's required. After planting, water thoroughly to settle the dirt around the roots and keep the soil moist for several weeks as the new plant grows.

Mulch around the base of the plant with organic mulch or leaf mulch, but keep it away from the roots.

How to Care Bird's Nest Fern

Providing enough warmth, humidity, and moisture to a healthy bird's nest fern is crucial. One of the finest places to install a bird's nest fern as a houseplant is near a shower or tub in a bathroom, where it will receive maximum humidity and warmth, though it must also have a light source.

The plant's core section, which resembles a bird's nest, will produce new leaves on a regular basis. As the fresh, fragile fronds emerge from the center, do not touch, move, or manipulate them. They are exceedingly delicate, and if you touch them, you run the risk of damaging or deforming them.

- **Light**

In filtered sunlight to a modest amount of shade, bird's nest ferns thrive. Except for the extremely early morning sun, don't expose them to direct sunlight. Direct sunlight can cause the leaves to burn. An east- or north-facing window is great for indoors.

Depending on the weather, water deeply once or twice a week until the plant is established.

Place a little amount of Yates Dynamic Lifter Soil Improver & Plant Fertilizer directly into the center of the fern on an as-needed basis.

Grow Birds Nest Ferns in a Pot

Select a pot that is at least twice the size of the plant you've chosen. Position in the garden that gets part shadow to the filtered sun and is shaded from the afternoon sun.

Fill the pot halfway with Yates Potting Mix with Dynamic Lifter, a high-quality potting mix.

Take the plant out of its container and gently tease the roots.

Backfill the hole with potting mix, gradually firming it down. There is water in the well.

Mulch around the base of the plant with organic mulch or leaf mulch, but keep it away from the roots.

Depending on the weather, water deeply once or twice a week until the plant is established.

Place a little amount of Yates Dynamic Lifter Soil Improver & Plant Fertilizer directly into the center of the fern on an as-needed basis.

- **Soil**

These plants prefer soil that is loose, rich in organic materials and drains well. Container plants benefit from a peat-based potting mix.

- **Water**

The ferns prefer a regular level of soil moisture, but they do not thrive in wet soil. When the top inch of soil is dry, water it. Avoid watering the plant directly in the center, as this might foster mold and rot in the dense nest. To prevent wetting the fern's fronds, aim water at the dirt.

- **Temperature and Humidity**

Temperatures between 60 and 80 degrees Fahrenheit are ideal for the bird's nest fern. It can withstand temperatures as low as 50 degrees Fahrenheit, but anything colder than that can kill the plant, especially if exposed for an extended period of time. Indoors, keep your plant away from cool draughts like those coming from an air conditioner vent. High humidity and damp conditions, such as a bathroom, greenhouse, or terrarium, are ideal for this fern. A humidifier can be used to increase the humidity surrounding a bird's nest fern. You can also place its pot on a tray with rocks and water. However, make sure the pot's bottom isn't submerged in water, as this can cause root rot.

- **Fertilizer**

Fertilize the fern once a month with a balanced liquid fertilizer diluted to half-strength throughout the active growing season (April through September). Make sure the fertilizer is applied to the soil rather than the fronds, as direct contact with the fertilizers can cause foliage to burn. Withhold fertilizer for the remainder of the year because too much food might cause the fronds to wilt or turn a yellowish or brownish tint.

Propagation of Bird Nest Fern

The bird's nest fern is a popular and appealing fern that defies common fern preconceptions. This plant features long, solid fronds with a crinkly appearance around their edges, rather than the feathery, segmented leaves commonly associated with ferns. It takes its name from the plant's crown, or center, which looks like a bird's nest. It's an epiphyte, which means it grows on other objects rather than on the ground, such as trees. So, how do you get one of these ferns to grow? Continue reading to learn how to extract spores from ferns and how to propagate spores from bird's nest ferns.

- **Collecting Spores from Bird's Nest Ferns**

Bird's nest ferns reproduce through spores, which appear on the undersides of the fronds as small brown dots. Remove a frond and place it in a paper bag when the spores on it are plump and fuzzy looking. The spores should fall off the front and gather in the bottom of the bag during the next few days. Propagation of Bird's Nest Fern Spores Sphagnum moss, or peat moss combined with dolomite, is ideal for propagating bird's nest spores. Place the spores on top of the growing media but do not cover them. Place the pot in a dish of water and let it soak up the water from the bottom.

It's critical to keep the spores of your bird's nest fern moist. You have the option of covering your pot with plastic wrap or a plastic bag or leaving it uncovered and misting it regularly. If you choose to cover the pot, do so after 4 to 6 weeks. Place the pot in a shady location. The spores should germinate in about two weeks if kept between 70 and 80 degrees Fahrenheit (21-27 degrees Celsius). The ferns thrive in low light and high humidity at 70 to 90 degrees Fahrenheit (21-32 C).

Rubber Plants

Ficus elastica is another name for a rubber tree. These massive trees can reach heights of 50 feet (15 meters). There are a few crucial things to consider when learning how to care for a rubber tree plant, but it isn't as tough as it may appear. Starting with a young rubber tree houseplant will allow it to better adapt to an indoor plant than a more established one.

The evergreen tropical tree ficuselastica is native to southern China, Southeast Asia, and Indonesia. It is a member of the Moraceae family of plants, and its latex sap was used to create rubber until synthetics became accessible. Hevea brasiliensis, on the other hand, produces the majority of natural rubber. Although many plants contain significant amounts of isoprene, these two species have enough in their latexy sap to manufacture rubber.

Ficus elastica roots are used to build live bridges in tropical Northeastern India, in addition to being helpful for rubber! The ficus elastica roots are led along a dead tree trunk that has been placed over a river. The roots grow to the other side of the trunk as it rots, thickening and training new roots to complete the bridge. Because it is flexible, the bridge can withstand strong winds and flooding. This tree is very stretchy in more ways than one! Rubber trees are ideal houseplants since they are low-light tolerant and assist in purifying the air.

Moraceae is a plant family that includes shrubs, trees, and lianas that all leak a latexy sap when cut. Foliar polymorphisms are found in members of this family, which means that the shape of their leaves varies depending on their life stage. Most other plants produce the same leaf forms throughout their lifetimes. Therefore this is a peculiar feature.

How to Grow Rubber Plants

Choose a pot that is no more than 1/3 times the size of your plant's root ball.

Fill it up to a third of the way with Miracle indoor Potting Mix. Since of its particular composition, this mix is great for rubber plants because it drains effectively, provides for optimum air circulation, and holds and releases water as needed.

Wear gloves and a long-sleeved shirt before planting to protect yourself in case a stem breaks. Some people may be irritated by the milky latex it contains.

So that the dirt doesn't overflow when you water the plant, place it in the container with the top of the root ball about an inch below the rim.

How to Care Rubber Plant

While rubber plants are a hardy variety, they require some special attention to achieve the appropriate balance in their surroundings. That requires plenty of sunshine, moist (but not soggy) soil, and enough fertilizer to keep it alive and well.

The waxy-looking leaves of the rubber plant start off pink-coral in color before developing to dark rich green. As the rubber plant matures, it will begin to droop, so you'll need to support it with a long wooden dowel (or bamboo stalk) to keep it upright.

- **Light**

Rubber plants, like most plants in their genus, thrive in bright, diffused light. They

More soil must be added around the root ball.

Water until the liquid at the bottom of the pot begins to drain.

Place a saucer under the pot and transfer your rubber plant to its new location.

Where to Grow Rubber Plants

While rubber plants thrive in bright, indirect light (such as that provided by south- or west-facing windows), they can also thrive in lower light, making them ideal office plants. Aside from the fact that bright, direct light might sunburn them, they aren't fussy about light. Rubber plants are tropical plants that don't appreciate being stuck with chilly blasts of air from doors or draughty windows, and if they are, they may drop some leaves.

Rubber plants can be grown outside in both sunny and shaded regions if you live in zones 10 through 12. Rubber trees grow in rich, well-draining soil can grow to be quite large (20 to 30 feet tall), so make sure you place them where they can spread out a bit—or cut them.

can withstand soft early sunlight but should be moved out of direct sunlight in the afternoon to avoid singeing the leaves. Plants that don't get enough light to grow leggy lose their bottom leaves, and their leaf color fades instead of becoming glossy and vivid.

- **Soil**

Rubber plants aren't choosy when it comes to soil composition. Any decent, fast-draining potting soil will usually suffice; however, many indoor gardeners prefer a cactus mix. Rubber plants also prefer an acidic soil composition. They, like fiddle leaf fig trees (which they are often mistaken for), "devour" their soil and finally reveal their roots. If this happens, simply add more soil to your container, and the problem will be solved.

- **Water**

Water your rubber plant on a regular basis; it prefers to be kept damp but not drenched. Rubber plants are also susceptible to drought and do not tolerate it well. Check the moisture levels in the first few inches of soil to see if it's time for another watering. If they're dry and crumbly, it's time to water your plant again.

- **Temperature and Humidity**

These plants, like other varieties of ficus trees, are susceptible to cool draughts. Unhealthy plants will become leggy with extending internodes, and their leaves will become yellow, brown, and eventually fall off. Rubber trees thrive in mild to warm temperatures between 60 and 75 degrees Fahrenheit, with moderate humidity. If your home is dry, consider purchasing a space humidifier to enhance the humidity levels.

- **Fertilizer**

Throughout the growing season, feed the plant a mild liquid fertilizer. When they're in good health, they eat a lot. Some experts advise merely mildly fertilizing indoor plants to avoid them stretching and getting root-bound as a result of their rapid growth.

Propagation of Rubber Plant

Rubber trees, also known as Ficus elastica, are notoriously difficult to propagate and prune. You'll understand what we're talking about if you have one. When cut, they emit a milky fluid that leaks everywhere. Be aware that this sap is difficult to remove and is sticky and unpleasant.

You'll need

- An established Rubber tree (no babies)
- Paper towels
- Rooting hormone
- A clean surface
- A gallon zip-top bag
- A pair of sharp pruners
- A small pot with filled with a 50/50 mix of gardening soil and perlite

Now, let's jump in

Pick the stem

Choose a stem that is healthy and has healthy leaves. On Rudy, We chose a leggy stem that didn't get much sun and could use some pruning.

Conclusion

Plants in the house are a lovely compliment to any room. However, when choosing indoor plants, keep in mind the conditions in which they will be grown. For plants to thrive, they must have adequate light, temperature, and humidity and be placed in an appropriate location. If you keep these things in good shape, your interior will look fantastic all year.

Plants are critical because they form the foundation of all life on Earth and are vital for humans. They give food, air, shelter, and medication and assist in the distribution and purification of water. Make careful to honor the world's plants and contribute to their preservation.